HAPPY 40TH!

(name of person receiving book)

Get ready for a super fun trip down memory lane! Inside this book, you'll find activities designed to spark smiles as you travel back in time.

We'll revisit trendy styles and pop culture from your era with some friendly trivia. You'll get to journal about monumental events and where you were when they happened. We'll reflect on your favorite moments both big and small - everything that's shaped your life story.

Go at your own pace, writing or just thinking about the good times. Stick in photos that capture memories. Most importantly, have fun reliving it all!

Your memories and wisdom need to be shared. Future generations would love to learn from your experiences. So grab a comfy seat and a nice pen, and start your stroll down memory lane. Everything about you is worth remembering.

CHEERS TO FORTY!

From Numbers to Narratives: 40 Years of Living!

40 TRIPS AROUND THE SUN
480 MONTHS
14,610 DAYS
350,640 HOURS
1,262,304,000 SECONDS

Go ahead and calculate these for yourself!

Number of homes you've lived in.. ☐

Number of times you've fallen in love... ☐

Number of cars you've owned.. ☐

Number of jobs.. ☐

Number of schools attended.. ☐

Number of pets loved... ☐

Number of languages learned.. ☐

Number of countries visited... ☐

Number of states visited... ☐

Where Were You?

Where were you and what were you doing during these momentous events?

1. The O.J. Simpson Car Chase and Trial (1994):

2. Princess Diana's Death (1997):

3. Columbine High School shooting (1999)

4. 9/11 Attacks (2001):

5. The Iraq War Begins (2003):

6. Hurricane Katrina (2005):

7. SpaceX's First Successful Rocket Launch (2008):

8. Election of First Black president (2008):

9. The Royal Wedding of Prince William and Kate Middleton (2011):

10. Capitol Riot on January 6th (2021):

What other events are seared in your memory?

SHORT & SWEET

✦ 20 QUESTIONS ✦

1. Full name: _____

2. Place of birth: _____

3. Number of siblings: _____

4. First time to see the ocean: _____

5. First book you remember: _____

6. First vacation: _____

7. First meal you learned to cook: _____

8. First fast food restaurant: _____

9. First pet: _____

10. First movie you remember: _____

11. First best friend: _____

12. First boy/girl went steady with: _____

13. First kiss: _____

14. First love: _____

15. First plane ride: _____

16. First car: _____

17. First job: _____

18. First concert attended: _____

19. First home: _____

20. First big item you saved up to purchase: _____

SHORT & SWEET

✦ 20 FAVORITES ✦

1. Favorite decade: _____

2. Favorite family vacation: _____

3. Favorite games as a child: _____

4. Favorite movie: _____

5. Favorite classic car: _____

6. Favorite meal: _____

7. Favorite dessert: _____

8. Favorite hairstyle: _____

9. Favorite tv show: _____

10. Favorite candy: _____

11. Favorite teacher: _____

12. Favorite book: _____

13. Favorite quote: _____

14. Favorite job: _____

15. Favorite scent: _____

16. Favorite age: _____

17. Favorite holiday: _____

18. Favorite family story: _____

19. Favorite childhood song: _____

20. Favorite dance craze: _____

FASHIONISTA

How many different fashion trends did you rock?

Early to Mid-1990s (Ages 10-16):
____ **Grunge Fashion:** Flannels, ripped jeans, and band T-shirts.
____ **Hip-Hop Style:** Baggy jeans, oversized shirts, and brand names like FUBU and Tommy Hilfiger become popular.
____ **Minimalist Trends:** Simple lines and colors, counteracting the bright and bold styles of the late 80s.
____ **Skater Culture:** Fashion with brands like Vans and graphic tees.

Late 1990s to Early 2000s (Ages 16-22):
____ **Y2K Aesthetics:** Metallics, futuristic designs, and tech-inspired accessories.
____ **Pop Star Influence:** Inspired by pop icons like Britney Spears and Christina Aguilera - low-rise jeans, crop tops, and flashy accessories.
____ **Emo and Scene Trends:** Skinny jeans, band tees, studded belts, and Converse shoes.

Mid to Late 2000s (Ages 22-26):
____ **Indie and Hipster:** Vintage-inspired looks, skinny jeans, and quirky accessories.
____ **Boho-Chic Revival:** Flowy dresses, ethnic prints, and natural materials, popularized by celebrities like Sienna Miller and Kate Moss.
____ **Athleisure Emergence:** The blending of athletic wear with leisure wear, leading to the popularity of yoga pants and sporty tops as everyday clothing.
____ **Fast Fashion Boom:** Affordable, trend-driven fashion from brands like Forever 21, H&M and Zara.

Early 2010s (Ages 26-30):
____ **Normcore and Minimalism:** Understated, unbranded clothing.
____ **High-Low Fashion Mix:** High-end designer items with fast fashion and vintage.
____ **Sustainable Fashion:** Eco-friendly and ethically made clothing.
____ **Color Blocking:** Using bold and contrasting hues.
____ **Statement Accessories:** Oversized sunglasses, chunky jewelry, large scarves, and statement hats.

____ **TOTAL** *Which fashion trends do you wish were still around today?*

HAIRSTYLES

How many of these hairstyles have you had?

1990s (Childhood to Teen - Ages 7-16):
____ **Curtain Bangs:** Inspired by teen idols like Leonardo DiCaprio.
____ **High Ponytails and Scrunchies:** Influenced by pop culture icons like the Spice Girls.
____ **Hi-top Fades:** Inspired by hip-hop culture.
____ **Box Braids and Beaded Braids:** Popularized by celebrities and musicians, adopted widely across various communities.

Early 2000s (Late Teens to Early 20s):
____ **Spiky Hair:** Using gel to create textured, edgy looks.
____ **Straightened Hair with Flat Irons:** Often with chunky highlights.
____ **Layered Haircuts:** "Flippy" hairdos inspired by pop-punk bands and celebrities.

Late 2000s to Early 2010s (Mid 20s to Early 30s):
____ **Emo Hair:** Long side-swept bangs, often dyed black or with streaks of color.
____ **The "Scene" Look:** Teased hair with bold colors and asymmetrical cuts.
____ **Sleek Bob Cuts:** Chic and straight, often with a side parting.
____ **Man Bun:** Gaining popularity among men, along with well-groomed beards.

Mid to Late 2010s (Mid 30s):
____ **Balayage and Ombre Hair Colors:** Subtle, natural-looking dye techniques.
____ **Undercuts for Both Genders:** Shaved sides with longer hair on top.
____ **Lobs (Long Bobs):** Sometimes with beachy waves.

Early 2020s (Late 30s to Present):
____ **Textured Pixie Cuts:** Short, stylish, and easy to maintain.
____ **Soft, Natural Waves:** Moving away from overly styled hair to more natural, effortless looks.
____ **Blended Gray:** Stylishly embracing natural gray hair, often blended with subtle coloring techniques for a more natural transition.

____ **Total** *Which hairstyle was your favorite?* ....

HAVE YOU EVER?

Check off the items you have done.

- [ ] Gone scuba diving
- [ ] Learned an instrument
- [ ] Played Tetris on a Gameboy
- [ ] Fallen in love
- [ ] Been to a drive-in movie
- [ ] Ridden in a hot air balloon
- [ ] Sold items door to door
- [ ] Participated in a protest
- [ ] Run a marathon
- [ ] Been on television
- [ ] Lived abroad
- [ ] Performed in a school play
- [ ] Gone backpacking

- [ ] Worn a letter jacket
- [ ] Seen the northern lights
- [ ] Hitchhiked or picked up a hitchhiker
- [ ] Danced the Cha Cha Slide
- [ ] Learned another language
- [ ] Been in a dance contest
- [ ] Volunteered
- [ ] Owned a Lite Brite
- [ ] Locked your keys in the car
- [ ] Played the Legend of Zelda
- [ ] Met a celebrity
- [ ] Fought in a war
- [ ] Worn jellies

WOULD YOU RATHER?

Make your choices and then grab a friend or family member and ask them these questions to see how well they know you.

○ Wake up early	**OR**	Stay up late ○
○ Go shopping	**OR**	Shop online ○
○ Read a book	**OR**	Watch movie ○
○ Drink coffee	**OR**	Drink tea ○
○ Go to a party	**OR**	Quiet evening at home ○
○ Go on a cruise	**OR**	Go camping ○
○ Ice cream	**OR**	Pie ○
○ Cat person	**OR**	Dog person ○
○ Play board games	**OR**	Watch TV ○
○ Beach	**OR**	Mountains ○
○ Call	**OR**	Text ○
○ Travel the world	**OR**	Explore locally ○

THE PRICE IS RIGHT

How much did things cost back in 1984? Circle your best guess.

Avg. Wage/Year
a) $21,600
b) $10,200
c) $50,000

New Home
a) $150,500
b) $25,300
c) $86,730

New Car
a) $5,000
b) $9,350
c) $15,500

Gold/Ounce
a) $200
b) $360
c) $10

Gallon of Gas
a) $1.13
b) $0.55
c) $0.90

Harvard Tuition
a) $2,000
b) $400
c) $9,500

Personal Computer
a) $15,000
b) $2,495
c) $1,500

Postage Stamp
a) $0.05
b) $0.20
c) $0.10

A Movie Ticket
a) $1.25
b) $0.10
c) $2.50

** costs are average estimates
(check your answers on page 38)*

YOUNGER OR OLDER?

Do you think you're younger or older than these inventions?

		Younger	Older
1	**Microwave oven**	○	○
2	**Tupperware**	○	○
3	**Game Boy**	○	○
4	**DVD**	○	○
5	**Color TV**	○	○
6	**Prozac**	○	○
7	**Disposable Contact Lenses**	○	○
8	**Hula Hoop**	○	○
9	**Google**	○	○
10	**Car Seat Belts**	○	○
11	**Barbie Doll**	○	○
12	**Windows 1.0**	○	○
13	**Post-It Note**	○	○
14	**Handheld Calculator**	○	○
15	**Sliced Bread**	○	○

(check your answers on page 39)

WORD SEARCH

W	A	L	K	M	A	N	C	H	L
M	M	A	R	R	A	M	B	O	L
A	T	H	P	R	T	A	I	Y	A
N	V	L	V	V	A	D	B	N	W
E	S	E	I	N	O	O	G	I	N
R	V	C	I	G	N	N	N	R	I
A	H	H	N	R	B	N	I	V	L
C	S	E	E	R	A	A	R	A	R
A	N	H	N	A	M	T	V	N	E
M	C	R	E	L	P	P	A	A	B

MTV   ATARI   CHERNOBYL

MACARENA   NIRVANA   MADONNA

APPLE   GOONIES   RAMBO

BERLIN WALL   VHS   WALKMAN

(check your answers on page 40)

GUESS THE MOVIE

Draw a line to match the movie each quote comes from.

"You're killing me Smalls!"

The Princess Bride, 1987

"Inconceivable!"

The Sandlot, 1993

"Never give up on yourself."

Ghostbusters, 1984

"Who you gonna call?"

Jumanji, 1995

"Welcome to the jungle!"

The NeverEnding Story, 1984

"If you build it, they will come."

Indiana Jones and the Temple of Doom, 1984

"I'll be back."

The Terminator, 1984

"Wax on, wax off."

The Karate Kid, 1984

"We're going to need a bigger boat."

Field of Dreams, 1988

(check your answers on page 41)

BORN IN 1984

True or false. Guess which people were born in 1984.

		True	False
1	LeBron James	○	○
2	Omarion	○	○
3	Ryan Gosling	○	○
4	Mark Zuckerberg	○	○
5	Jennifer Lawrence	○	○
6	Katy Perry	○	○
7	Reese Witherspoon	○	○
8	Avril Lavigne	○	○
9	Beyoncé	○	○
10	Scarlett Johansson	○	○
11	Katharine McPhee	○	○
12	Prince Harry	○	○
13	Lady Gaga	○	○
14	Taylor Swift	○	○
15	Mandy Moore	○	○

(check your answers on page 42)

1980s SLANG

Draw a line to match.

1. **Booyah**
2. **Chillin'**
3. **Da bomb**
4. **Fly**
5. **Hella**
6. **Ice**
7. **Jiggy**
8. **Peace out**
9. **Whatever**
10. **My bad**
11. **Dibs**
12. **Mad props**
13. **As if!**
14. **Baller**
15. **Wicked sick**

Hanging out

Express excitement or victory

used to emphasize somethin

Express disbelief or sarcasm

Indifference or lack of interest

Cool or fashionable

Diamonds or bling

To apologize for something

Very good or awesome

To dance or to party

Say goodbye

Admiration or respect for someone's achievements

Good at something, especially sports

Claim something as yours

Extreme enthusiasm or approval

(check your answers on page 43)

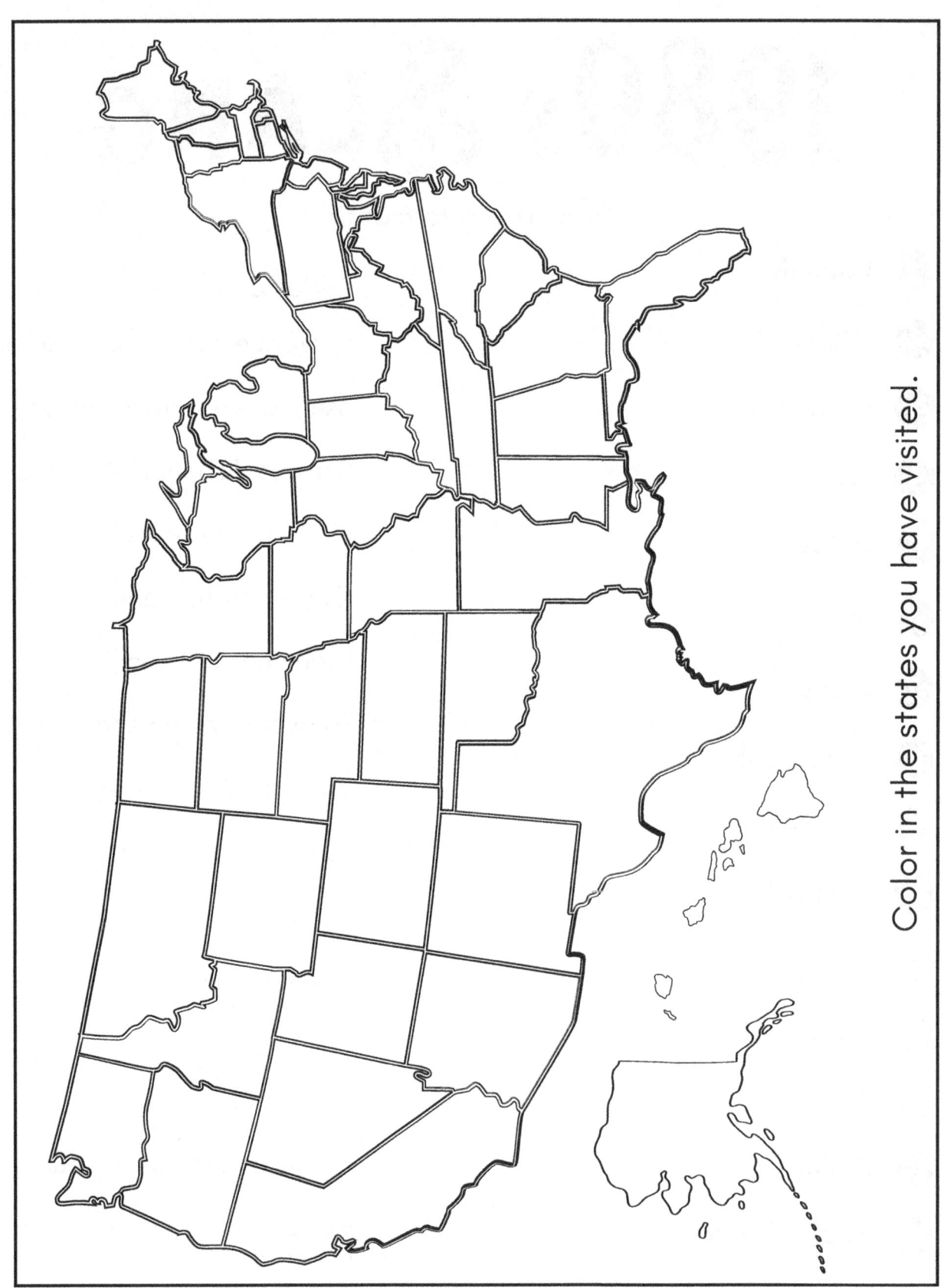

Color in the states you have visited.

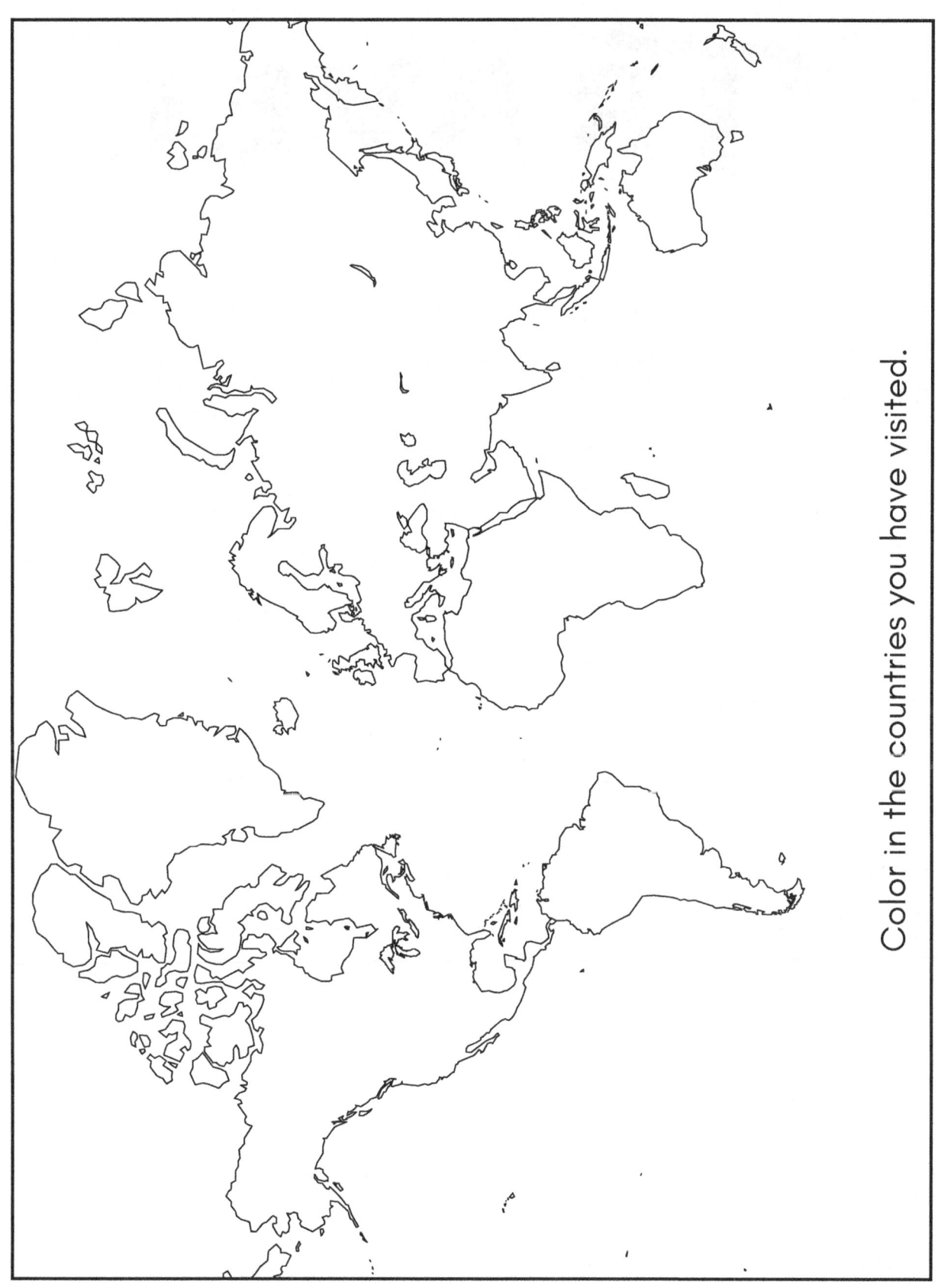

Color in the countries you have visited.

TRAVEL

When: _____ Where: _____

Who was with you: _____

Things you saw: _____

_____

_____

Things you did: _____

_____

_____

One part of the trip you *wish* you could repeat: _____

When: _____ Where: _____

Who was with you: _____

Things you saw: _____

_____

_____

Things you did: _____

_____

_____

One part of the trip you *wish* you could repeat: _____

TRAVEL

When: .... Where: ....

Who was with you: ....

Things you saw: ....

....

....

Things you did: ....

....

....

One part of the trip you *wish* you could repeat: ....

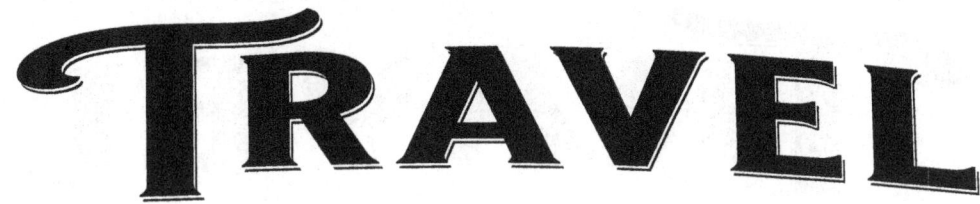

When: .... Where: ....

Who was with you: ....

Things you saw: ....

....

....

Things you did: ....

....

....

One part of the trip you *wish* you could repeat: ....

TRAVEL

When: _____ Where: _____

Who was with you: _____

Things you saw: _____

_____

_____

Things you did: _____

_____

_____

One part of the trip you *wish* you could repeat: _____

When: _____ Where: _____

Who was with you: _____

Things you saw: _____

_____

_____

Things you did: _____

_____

_____

One part of the trip you *wish* you could repeat: _____

TRAVEL

When: .... Where: ....

Who was with you: ....

Things you saw: ....

....

....

Things you did: ....

....

....

One part of the trip you *wish* you could repeat: ....

When: .... Where: ....

Who was with you: ....

Things you saw: ....

....

....

Things you did: ....

....

....

One part of the trip you *wish* you could repeat: ....

CHALLENGE

Quick recall - no searching for answers!

How many Madonna songs can you name?

How many cartoon characters can you name from the 80s and 90s?

How many wars from when you were born to now can you name?

How many different dance crazes from the past can you recall attempting?

How many countries can you name that changed their names in your lifetime?

How many Vice Presidents from when you were born to now can you name?

How many classic TV shows from the 80s and 90s can you name?

How many schoolyard games from your childhood can you remember?

How many famous musicals from your era can you name?

Head to the internet to dive deeper and check your answers!

FINISH THE SENTENCE

Do your best to finish the lyrics of these iconic songs.

"Sweet dreams are made of this, _____."
- Eurythmics, "Sweet Dreams (Are Made of This)" (1983)

"Smells like teen spirit, _____." - Nirvana,
"Smells Like Teen Spirit" (1991)

"We're livin' on a prayer, take my hand, _____."
- Bon Jovi, "Livin' on a Prayer" (1986)

"Wannabe, if you wanna be my lover, you gotta _____."
- Spice Girls, "Wannabe" (1996)

"Like a virgin, _____."
- Madonna, "Like a Virgin" (1984)

"Waterfalls, _____, please stick to the
rivers and the lakes that you're used to..." - TLC, "Waterfalls" (1994)

"Genie in a Bottle, I'm a genie in a bottle, _____."
- Christina Aguilera, "Genie in a Bottle" (1999)

"I Don't Want to Miss a Thing, _____."
- Aerosmith, "I Don't Want to Miss a Thing" (1998)

"Wake me up _____, don't leave me hanging on like a
yo-yo." - Wham! (1984)

"I want to dance with somebody, _____ with
somebody." - Whitney Houston (1987)

(check your answers on page 44)

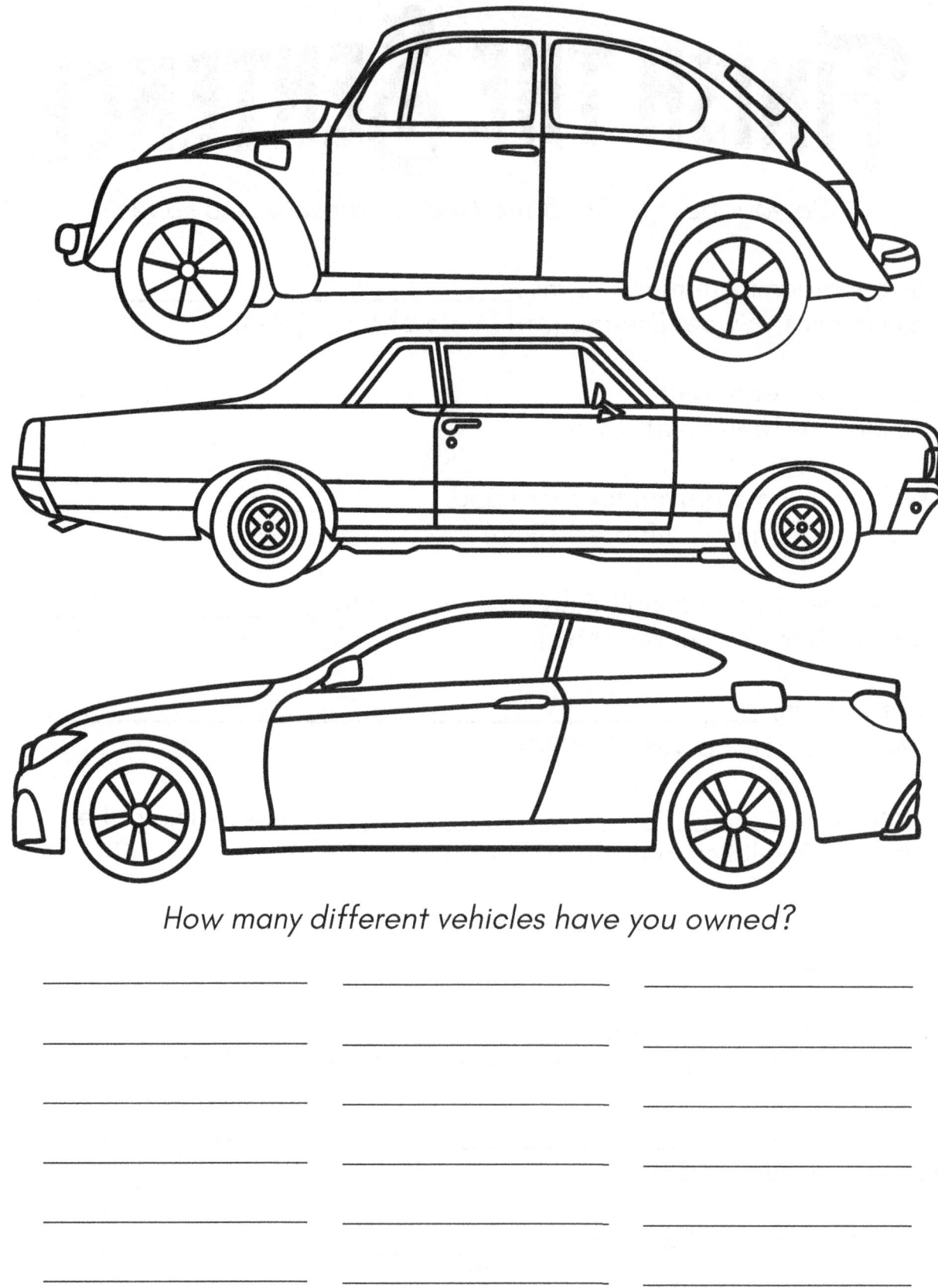

How many different vehicles have you owned?

_____ _____ _____

_____ _____ _____

_____ _____ _____

_____ _____ _____

_____ _____ _____

_____ _____ _____

In 1872, Walter Scott pioneered the first diner concept by selling food from a horse-pulled wagon with walk-up service windows in Providence, Rhode Island.

Did you have a favorite diner? If so, where was it?

PRESIDENTS

Review the pictures of the presidents elected in your lifetime.
*Color in the ones **you or your parents** voted for.*

Ronald Reagan
1981 – 1989

George H.W. Bush
1989 – 1993

Bill Clinton
1993 – 2001

George W. Bush
2001 – 2009

Barack Obama
2009 – 2017

Donald Trump
2017 – 2021

Joe Biden
2021

NOSTALGIA NOTES

Fill in the blanks first, then go back and read your story aloud.

Way back in_____, I landed my first job as a
(favorite year)

_____. It was as exhilarating as my first roller coaster ride
(first job)

at _____. Every day, I'd hop into my trusty _____,
(first vacation spot)   (first car)

with _____ by my side, barking along to the tunes
(first pet's name)

of_____. Work was a far cry from _____,
(favorite song)   (favorite hobby)

but it paid for my _____ addiction and movie nights
(favorite dessert)

featuring _____.
(favorite actor/actress)

One evening, after a long shift, I mustered the courage to ask

_____ out on a date. We planned to meet at
(first date's name)

_____. I put on my _____, which I thought was
(favorite restaurant)   (item of clothing)

the epitome of cool. Unfortunately, the _____ was so tight;
(article of clothing)

it made sitting down a risky business! During dinner, I tried to

impress with stories about my _____, but
(a life accomplishment)

accidentally spat out a piece of _____ right onto the
(favorite food)

_____. Despite the mishap, we ended up having a blast,
(an object in a kitchen)

laughing like we were characters in _____.
(your favorite book)

It was a night to remember!

-29-

Remember When

*Instead of focusing on the year you were born, let's focus on the years you remember! While the year you were born is important, it's the years after that defined who you are today. Let's take a trip along the journey and discover **why you are who you are.***

1992 - You turned 8
The release of the popular video game "Super Mario Kart" for the Super Nintendo Entertainment System.

Do you remember the first video game you played? How did video games help shape your childhood?

1994 - You turned 10
The release of "The Lion King," one of Disney's most popular animated films, known for its memorable music and story.

Recall the first time you watched "The Lion King." What impact did it have on you? Did you have favorite characters or songs?

REMEMBER WHEN

1997 - You turned 13
The death of Princess Diana, a moment that generated global attention and mourning.

Reflect on where you were and how you felt when you heard about Princess Diana's passing.

2000 - You turned 16
The turn of the millennium – the year 2000 was greeted with widespread celebrations and some anxieties (like the Y2K bug).

Think back to the New Year's Eve of 1999. How did you celebrate? Were you and your family or friends concerned about Y2K?

2002 - You turned 30
The widespread popularity of social media platforms began with the launch of Friendster, followed by Myspace.

Recall your first experiences with social media. How did these platforms change your interactions with friends?

REMEMBER WHEN

2005 - You turned 21
YouTube was launched, changing the way people consumed and shared video content.

Reflect on your initial encounters with YouTube. How did this platform influence your media consumption?

2009 - You turned 25
The inauguration of Barack Obama as the first African-American President of the United States.

Think about your thoughts and feelings regarding this election and inauguration. How did this historic event shape your views on politics and society?

2014 - You turned 30
The ALS Ice Bucket Challenge goes viral on social media, raising awareness and funds for amyotrophic lateral sclerosis research.

Have you participated in any viral trends or social media challenges?

REMEMBER WHEN

2024 – You turn 40!

As you celebrate this milestone, what recent event has given you hope or excitement for the future?

More Milestone Memories

Make a note of any other major events or years that are seared in your memory as significant.

REFLECTIONS

Reflect on a moment of significant change in your life. If you could write to yourself just before this event, what insights or comfort would you offer?

Reflect on your career path or life's work. What would you say to your younger self about following their dreams and the realities of the working world?

Recall a time you took a significant risk. Encourage your younger self about the value of risk-taking and the growth that comes from stepping out of your comfort zones.

REFLECTIONS

Ponder on the love and relationships in your life. Offer your younger self wisdom about love, loss, and the enduring nature of true connections.

Think of a joyous milestone in your life. Tell your younger self about the happiness that lies ahead and the importance of savoring those moments.

Acknowledge the societal changes you've witnessed. Write about how these changes have shaped your perspective and the world you've navigated.

CHECK YOUR ANSWERS

THE PRICE IS RIGHT

Check your answers.

Avg. Wage/Year
a) $21,600 (circled)
b) $10,200
c) $50,000

New Home
a) $150,500
b) $25,300
c) $86,730 (circled)

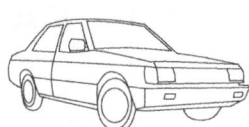

New Car
a) $5,000
b) $9,350 (circled)
c) $15,500

Gold/Ounce
a) $200
b) $360 (circled)
c) $10

Gallon of Gas
a) $1.13 (circled)
b) $0.55
c) $0.90

Harvard Tuition
a) $2,000
b) $400
c) $9,500 (circled)

Personal Computer
a) $15,000
b) $2,495 (circled)
c) $1,500

Postage Stamp
a) $0.05
b) $0.20 (circled)
c) $0.10

A Movie Ticket
a) $1.25
b) $0.10
c) $2.50 (circled)

costs are average estimates

YOUNGER OR OLDER?

Check your answers.

		Younger	Older
1	**Microwave oven**	✓ 1945	○
2	**Tupperware**	✓ 1946	○
3	**Game Boy**	○	✓ 1989
4	**DVD**	○	✓ 1995
5	**Color TV**	✓ 1953	○
6	**Prozac**	○	✓ 1987
7	**Disposable Contact Lenses**	○	✓ 1987
8	**Hula Hoop**	✓ 1957	○
9	**Google**	○	✓ 1998
10	**Car Seat Belts**	✓ 1855	○
11	**Barbie Doll**	✓ 1959	○
12	**Windows 1.0**	○	✓ 1985
13	**Post-It Note**	✓ 1968	○
14	**Handheld Calculator**	✓ 1967	○
15	**Sliced Bread**	✓ 1928	○

WORD SEARCH

W	A	L	K	M	A	N	C	H	L
M	M	A	R	R	A	M	B	O	L
A	T	H	P	R	T	A	I	Y	A
N	V	L	V	V	A	D	B	N	W
E	S	E	I	N	O	O	G	I	N
R	V	C	I	G	N	N	N	R	I
A	H	H	N	R	B	N	I	V	L
C	S	E	E	R	A	A	R	A	R
A	N	H	N	A	M	T	V	N	E
M	C	R	E	L	P	P	A	A	B

MTV **ATARI** **CHERNOBYL**

MACARENA **NIRVANA** **MADONNA**

APPLE **GOONIES** **RAMBO**

BERLIN WALL **VHS** **WALKMAN**

GUESS THE MOVIE

Check your answers.

"You're killing me Smalls!" — The Princess Bride, 1987

"Inconceivable!" — The Sandlot, 1993

"Never give up on yourself." — Ghostbusters, 1984

"Who you gonna call?" — Jumanji, 1995

"Welcome to the jungle!" — The NeverEnding Story, 1984

"If you build it, they will come." — Indiana Jones and the Temple of Doom, 1984

"I'll be back." — The Terminator, 1984

"Wax on, wax off." — The Karate Kid, 1984

"We're going to need a bigger boat." — Field of Dreams, 1988

BORN IN 1984

Check your answers.

		True	False
1	LeBron James	✓	
2	Omarion	✓	
3	Ryan Gosling		✓ (1980)
4	Mark Zuckerberg	✓	
5	Jennifer Lawrence		✓ (1989)
6	Katy Perry	✓	
7	Reese Witherspoon		✓ (1976)
8	Avril Lavigne	✓	
9	Beyoncé		✓ (1981)
10	Scarlett Johansson	✓	
11	Katharine McPhee	✓	
12	Prince Harry	✓	
13	Lady Gaga		✓ (1986)
14	Taylor Swift		✓ (1989)
15	Mandy Moore	✓	

1980s SLANG

Check your answers.

1 **Booyah** — Hanging out

2 **Chillin'** — Express excitement or victory

3 **Da bomb** — used to emphasize somethin

4 **Fly** — Express disbelief or sarcasm

5 **Hella** — Indifference or lack of interest

6 **Ice** — Cool or fashionable

7 **Jiggy** — Diamonds or bling

8 **Peace out** — To apologize for something

9 **Whatever** — Very good or awesome

10 **My bad** — To dance or to party

11 **Dibs** — Say goodbye

12 **Mad props** — Admiration or respect for someone's achievements

13 **As if!** — Good at something, especially sports

14 **Baller** — Claim something as yours

15 **Wicked sick** — Extreme enthusiasm or approval

FINISH THE SENTENCE

Check your answers.

"Sweet dreams are made of this, **who am I to disagree?**" - Eurythmics, "Sweet Dreams (Are Made of This)" (1983)

"Smells like teen spirit, **here we are now, entertain us.**" - Nirvana, "Smells Like Teen Spirit" (1991)

"We're livin' on a prayer, take my hand, **we'll make it I swear.**" - Bon Jovi, "Livin' on a Prayer" (1986)

"Wannabe, if you wanna be my lover, you gotta **get with my friends.**" - Spice Girls, "Wannabe" (1996)

"Like a virgin, **touched for the very first time.**" - Madonna, "Like a Virgin" (1984)

"Waterfalls, **don't go chasing waterfalls,** please stick to the rivers and the lakes that you're used to..." - TLC, "Waterfalls" (1994)

"Genie in a Bottle, I'm a genie in a bottle, **you gotta rub me the right way.**" - Christina Aguilera, "Genie in a Bottle" (1999)

"I Don't Want to Miss a Thing, **I could stay awake just to hear you breathing.**" - Aerosmith, "I Don't Want to Miss a Thing" (1998)

"Wake me up **before you go-go**, don't leave me hanging on like a yo-yo." - Wham! (1984)

"I want to dance with somebody, **I want to feel the heat** with somebody." - Whitney Houston (1987)

TIMELINE

Pause to thoughtfully record a few of the significant milestones and events that have shaped your journey.

Date: Event/Memory:

Date: Event/Memory:

Date: Event/Memory:

Date: Event/Memory:

Date: Event/Memory:

TIMELINE

Date: Event/Memory:

Date: Event/Memory:

Date: Event/Memory:

Date: Event/Memory:

Date: Event/Memory:

TIMELINE

Date: Event/Memory:

Date: Event/Memory:

Date: Event/Memory:

Date: Event/Memory:

Date: Event/Memory:

TIMELINE

Date: Event/Memory:

Date: Event/Memory:

Date: Event/Memory:

Date: Event/Memory:

Date: Event/Memory:

TIMELINE

Date: Event/Memory:

Date: Event/Memory:

Date: Event/Memory:

Date: Event/Memory:

Date: Event/Memory:

GRATITUDE

With 40 years worth of blessings, take a moment now to fill in your year of birth with the first things that spring to mind for which you are deeply grateful.

THE FUTURE

Anticipating the future, fill in the year 2024 with any goals and dreams that still remain on your bucket list.

NOTES

NOTES

49621770R00030